THE BILL & PEGGY CLAIR LITERARY FUND

Books for Young Readers

hundred thousands	ten thousands	thousands	hundreds	tens	ones	tenths	hundredths
9	0	1,	2	3	4.	5	6

For my author ally Kerri Kunkel—D. A. A.

To my mom—E. M.

Text copyright © 2016 by David A. Adler
Illustrations copyright © 2016 by Edward Miller
All Rights Reserved
HOLIDAY HOUSE is registered in the U.S. Patent and Trademark Office.
Printed and Bound in January 2016 at Worzalla, Stevens Point, WI, USA.
The artwork was created digitally.
www.holidayhouse.com
First Edition
1 3 5 7 9 10 8 6 4 2

Library of Congress Cataloging-in-Publication Data

Adler, David A., author.
Place value / by David A. Adler ; illustrated by Edward Miller. — First edition.
pages cm
Summary: "The mathematical concept of place value is explained using a place value chart,
descriptions of how money is notated, and humorous examples from a recipe that a group of
monkeys is using to make a gigantic banana muffin."— Provided by publisher.
Audience: Ages 5-8.
Audience: K to grade 3.
ISBN 978-0-8234-3550-0 (hardcover)
1. Place value (Mathematics)—Juvenile literature. 2. Decimal system—Juvenile literature. 3.
Numeration—Juvenile literature. I. Miller, Edward, 1964- illustrator. II. Title.
QA141.3.A324 2016
513.2'1—dc23
2015014874

Visit www.davidaadler.com for more information on the author, for a list of his books and to download
teacher's guides and educational materials. You can also learn more about the writing process, take fun
quizzes and read select pages from David A. Adler's books.

PLACE VALUE

OPEN

BANANA CAFE

by David A. Adler • illustrated by Edward Miller

Holiday House / New York

A is both a **word** and a **letter**.

1 is both a **number** and a **digit**.

A is the first word in the sentence

"**A** frog jumped onto my cupcake."

A is the fifth letter in the word "cupc**a**ke."

1 is the number in the sentence

"We're number **1**."

1 is the second digit in the number **318**.

We write **words** with **letters**. There are **twenty-six letters** in our alphabet:

A, B, C, D, E, F, G, H, I, J, K, L, M, N, O, P, Q, R, S, T, U, V, W, X, Y and Z.

Count the letters in the word **banana**.

Banana is a **word** with **six letters**.

MENU

BANANA CUPCAKE

BANANA BREAD

BANANA PUDDING

BANANA CUSTARD

BANANA TART

ANA PIE

We write **numbers** with **digits**. There are **ten digits** in our number system:

1, 2, 3, 4, 5, 6, 7, 8, 9 and 0.

Count the digits in the number **5,432**.

5,432 is a number with **four digits**.

Recipe 5,432
Colossal Banana
Cupcake

216	white eggs
621	brown eggs
9,347	cups of sugar
7,493	cups of flour
654,321	lbs. of butter
2,426,782	bananas
lots of	sprinkles

FLOUR

Order is important with both words and numbers.
POT and TOP have the same letters, but because their order
is different the words are different.

I said, hand me a P-O-T, not a T-O-P!

CAFE and FACE have the same letters, but because their order
is different the words are different.

216 and 621 have the same digits, but because their order is different the numbers are different.

The place of each digit in a number determines its value.

The **6** in 21**6** means **6 ones**.

hundreds	tens	ones
2	1	6

The **6** in **621** means **6 hundreds**.

hundreds	tens	ones
6	2	1

Recipe 5,432
Colossal Banana
Cupcake

216	white eggs
621	brown eggs
9,347	cups of sugar
7,493	cups of flour
654,321	lbs. of butter
2,426,782	bananas
lots of	sprinkles

13

9,347 and 7,493 have the same digits, but because their order is different the numbers are different.

SUGAR

Recipe 5,432
Colossal Banana
Cupcake

216   white eggs
621   brown eggs
9,347 cups of sugar
7,493 cups of flour
654,321 lbs. of butter
2,426,782 bananas
lots of sprinkles

thousands,	hundreds	tens	ones
9,	**3**	**4**	**7**

The **7** in 9,34**7** means **7 ones**.

thousands,	hundreds	tens	ones
7,	4	9	3

The **7** in **7,493** means **7 thousands**.

Take a look at this chart. On it you can see the value of each digit in the number 654,321.

In the number 654,321 there is a **comma** after the 4. Commas are used to break large numbers into groups of three digits. The groups of three are counted to the left from the ones place. The commas make numbers easier to read.

The first group of three, 321, is read "three hundred twenty-one." The second group of three, 654, is read "six hundred fifty-four thousand."

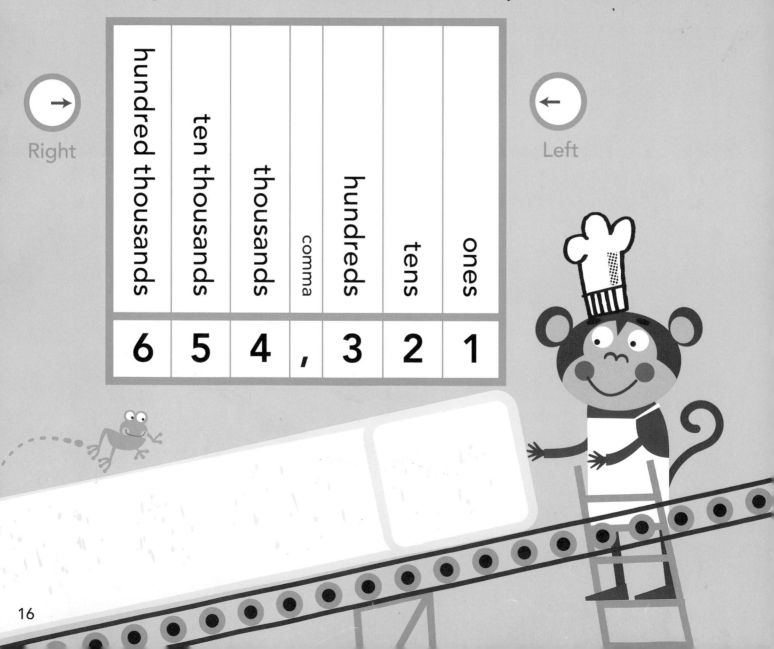

Right

Left

hundred thousands	ten thousands	thousands	comma	hundreds	tens	ones
6	5	4	,	3	2	1

With the ten digits in our number system we can write even larger numbers.

2,426,782 is a lot larger. 2,426,782 is read "two million, four hundred twenty-six thousand, seven hundred eighty-two."

The same digit **2** in the same number **2**,4**2**6,78**2** has three different values.

millions,	hundred thousands	ten thousands	thousands,	hundreds	tens	ones
2,	4	2	6,	7	8	2

From the left, the value of the first 2 is two million.
The value of the second 2 is twenty thousand.
The value of the third 2 is two.

19

Take a look at this place value chart.

hundreds	tens	ones	decimal point	tenths	hundredths
4	3	1	.	9	8

There's a dot to the right of the 1. That dot is a **decimal point**. It separates the columns of digits with values of **more than one** from those of **less than one**. Each column to the left of the decimal point is **ten times** more than the column before. Each column to the right is one-**tenth** of the column before. The value of the 9 to the right of the decimal point is nine-tenths — 9/10. The value of the 8 in the second column to right of the decimal point is eight-hundredths — 8/100.

Dollars, dimes and pennies can teach you about the decimal point.

How much money is in this box? If you write it in words, you write twelve dollars and thirty-four cents. If you write it as a number, you write $12.34.

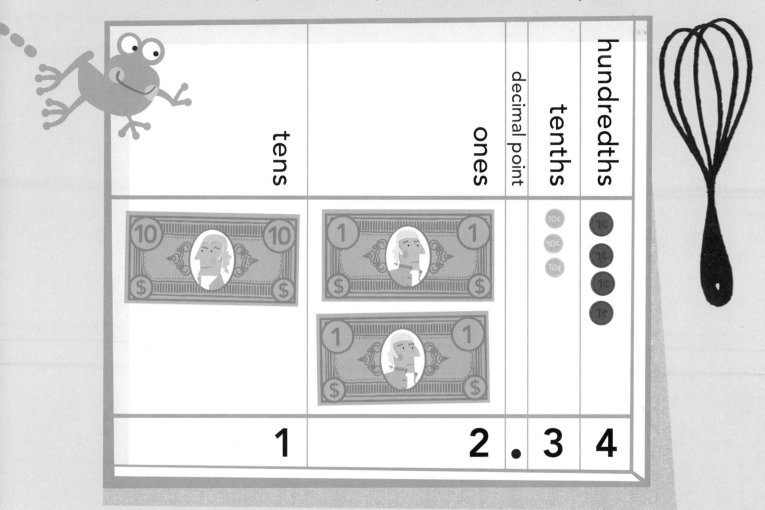

There is one ten-dollar bill in the box. The **1** in $**1**2.34 is in the **tens** place. It means ten dollars.

There are two one-dollar bills in the box. The **2** in $1**2**.34 is in the **ones** place. It means two dollars.

There are three dimes in the box. Each dime is one-tenth of a dollar. The **3** in $12.**3**4 is in the **tenths** place. It means three-tenths of a dollar.

There are four pennies in the box. Each penny is one-hundredth of a dollar. The **4** in $12.3**4** is in the **hundredths** place. It means four-hundredths of a dollar.

Our number system is called the Hindu-Arabic system. It was first developed in India a few thousand years ago and spread across the Middle East and to Europe. With just the ten symbols in the Hindu-Arabic system we can write any number no matter how large or how small. It's place value that makes our system so powerful.

Take another look at the place value chart.

millions	hundred thousands	ten thousands	thousands	hundreds	tens	ones	decimal point	tenths	hundredths
							•		

The first column to the right of the decimal point is for tenths.

The first column to the left of the decimal point is for any number less than ten.

The second column to the left is for tens.

The third column is for hundreds. Of course, each hundred is ten tens.

The fourth column is for thousands. Each thousand is ten hundreds and each hundred is ten tens.

Ten! Ten! Ten! Ten! Ten!

The Hindu-Arabic number system is based on ten. Why ten? Many people believe it's because we each have ten fingers.

Our number system may have started thousands of years ago when someone counted on his fingers. He reached ten and made a mark on the ground to show he had counted on all his fingers. The mark on the ground meant ten. He continued to count. Each time he counted all his fingers he made another mark. Each mark meant ten.

You know that 132 is not the same number as 123, and 123 is not the same number as 321. The digits in each of the numbers are the same, but the numbers are different.

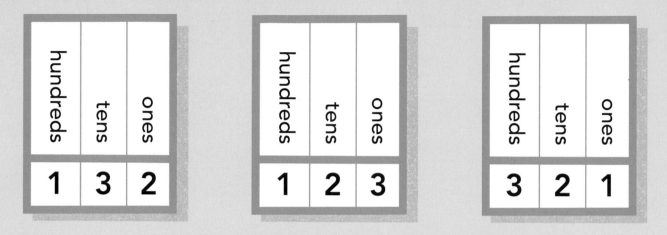

Our number system depends on place value. It's what enables us to write this huge number using just ten different digits: 329,465,180,708,643 — three hundred twenty-nine trillion, four hundred sixty-five billion, one hundred eighty million, seven hundred eight thousand, six hundred forty-three.

hundred trillions	ten trillions	trillions,	hundred billions	ten billions	billions,	hundred millions	ten millions	millions,	hundred thousands	ten thousands	thousands,	hundreds	tens	ones
3	2	9,	4	6	5,	1	8	0,	7	0	8,	6	4	3

329,465,180,708,643

Three hundred twenty nine- trillion!
That's a lot!

ten trillions

trillions ,

hundred billions

ten billions

billions ,

hundred millions

ten millions

millions ,

1 2, 3 4 5, 6 7 8,